BOSTON

A PICTORIAL SOUVENIR

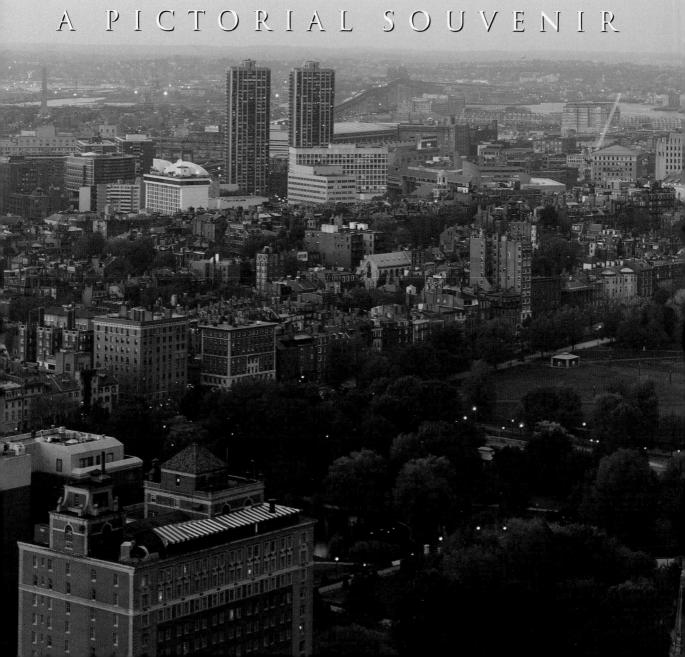

CAROL M. HIGHSMITH AND TED LANDPHAIR

BOSTON
A PICTORIAL SOUVENIR

CRESCENT BOOKS

NEW YORK

THE AUTHORS GRATEFULLY ACKNOWLEDGE
THE SERVICES, ACCOMMODATIONS, AND SUPPORT PROVIDED BY
HILTON HOTELS CORPORATION
IN CONNECTION WITH THE COMPLETION OF THIS BOOK.

———————

This 1997 edition is published by Crescent Books®,
an imprint of Random House Value Publishing, Inc.,
201 East 50th Street, New York, NY 10022.

Crescent Books® and design are registered trademarks of
Random House Value Publishing, Inc.

Random House
New York • Toronto • London • Sydney • Auckland
http://www.randomhouse.com/

Printed and bound in China

At dusk, the Boston
Common (pages
2–3)—the nation's
oldest public park,
covering fifty acres—
provides a muted
foreground for the
city's downtown
skyline. The capital
of Massachusetts is
not a city of notable
skyscrapers; it has
retained its human
scale and prides
itself on remaining
a "walking city."

Library of Congress Cataloging–in–Publication Data
Highsmith, Carol M., 1946–
Boston / Carol M. Highsmith and Ted Landphair.
p.   cm. — (A pictorial souvenir)
ISBN 0-517-20143-7
1. Boston (Mass.) — Pictorial works.   I. Landphair, Ted, 1942– .
II. Title.   III. Series: Highsmith, Carol M., 1946–   Pictorial souvenir.
F73.37.H49   1997   97-14050
974.4´61—dc21   CIP

8   7   6   5   4

———————

Project Editor: Donna Lee Lurker
Designed by Robert L. Wiser, Archetype Press, Inc., Washington, D.C.

FOREWORD

Boston, the nation's twentieth largest city and the Cradle of American Liberty, is an endlessly fascinating living-history museum of the seventeenth and eighteenth centuries. A proud and imposing colonial capital, it remains one of the country's preeminent walking cities today.

First settled in 1630 by John Winthrop and his band of Puritans, and originally occupying a sliver of land at the mouth of the Charles River, over the next two centuries the town continued to expand. As the city of Boston evolved, so did its landscape. Bostonians once clammed and fished in the estuary of the Charles River where the twenty-four-acre Public Garden, ruled forever public in an 1859 ordinance, now draws throngs of visitors. Replete with fountains, flower beds, and sculptures, the Public Garden is best loved for its twenty-passenger swan boats which ply its lagoon at a languorous pace. Commonwealth Avenue, a long and straight Victorian boulevard cutting across the Back Bay, was designed as an antidote to the tangle of streets found elsewhere in town. Its mall is graced with flowering magnolias, statues, and plenty of park benches. The nation's first subterranean streetcar—soon called a "subway"—opened underneath the Boston Common in 1897.

Indeed, Boston is a city of firsts. America's first significant port, first commercial center, and seedbed of its Revolution, Boston was also our first center of learning, and the first place where immigrants in large numbers disembarked. Boston relishes its role as the trustee of a good portion of America's colonial heritage, approaching modernity with caution. Even its visitors take comfort in knowing that they can leave Boston, perhaps for twenty years or more, and return to find most of the places they love still intact.

Photographers searching for a neatly packaged shot of the Boston skyline will be frustrated. Its tall buildings pop up in widely separated clusters, first downtown, in and around the Financial District, then on Beacon Hill. Boston's two loftiest structures, the Prudential Tower and the John Hancock Tower, loom off by themselves, a mile distant from downtown, on Boylston Street between the Back Bay and South End. Reflected in the Hancock Tower's glass are the buildings of historic Copley Square, including the sophisticated Copley Place mall, built in the early 1980s, old Trinity Church, and the magnificent Boston Public Library.

Elsewhere, the Museum of Science, a pioneer in "hand-on" education, maintains more than four hundred exhibits in anthropology, medicine, astronomy, and other sciences. The Computer Museum and the raucously enjoyable Children's Museum are housed in an old warehouse across the Congress Street Bridge on "Museum Wharf," where visitors to the Boston Tea Party Ship and Museum are invited to join in heaving bales of tea overboard. The New England Aquarium on Central Wharf features playful penguins, as well as a host of predators and other creatures from the briny deep. And, on the North End, Paul Revere's house, the only surviving building of seventeenth-century Boston, and an adjacent museum chronicling his life, are open to tours.

Boston—a city of the past which has created its own special present—is a treasure to be discovered and rediscovered by visitors and natives alike.

OVERLEAF: Beacon Hill and various office buildings rise above the Charles River.

Greek Revival is the architectural fashion in much of Beacon Hill's South Slope (opposite and left). When John Singleton Copley, a Tory sympathizer, fled to England after the Revolution, the Mount Vernon Properties syndicate purchased his land and built dozens of mansions and squares. While it bears no resemblance to the set of Cheers, on television, the Bull & Finch Pub on Beacon Street (above) inspired the long-running show. OVERLEAF: In the African Meeting House—known as the "Black Faneuil Hall"—on the Hill's North Slope, abolitionists railed against slavery. The building, which bears the scars of a devastating fire in 1973, is a featured stop on Boston's Black Heritage Trail.

"Ye Olde" Union Oyster House (opposite) dates to 1742, when it was Hopestill Capen's silk and dry-goods shop. In 1826 Atwood & Bacon installed the oyster bar and an open coal range and advertised itself as a fish house. The Old State House (left), Boston's oldest surviving public building, was the political center of the Massachusetts Bay Colony. Its lion and unicorn are symbols of the British Crown. Today it is a museum of Boston history. ABOVE: The 1848 Sears Block on City Hall Plaza retains Boston's most treasured sign— the 227-gallon (and two quarts, one pint, and three gills) steaming teakettle, moved from the demolished Scollay Square.

Hanover Street in front of Saint Stephen's Roman Catholic Church (opposite) is decked out for the Festival of Saint Agrippina. The 1804 church—another Charles Bulfinch creation—originally known as the New North Church, was a Congregationalist meetinghouse, then a Unitarian church, until it was sold to the Roman Catholic diocese in 1862. During the festival, church-men carry a decorated canopy (above) into which onlookers press donations. LEFT: Salem Street's many restaurants and pizzerias have maintained the Italian flavor of the city's North End. The area, which juts out into the Atlantic Ocean, was once called the "Island of North Boston" because a canal cut it off from the city.

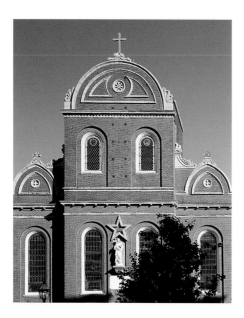

Sacred Heart Catholic Church (above) on North Square was originally a Protestant church with a large congregation of seafarers and their families. Nearby on the congested square is Paul Revere's house (right), which the silversmith—and maker of false teeth— bought in 1770 when it was already almost a century old. Its over- hanging second story, called a "jetty," typifies the frame construction of the period, follow- ing the devastating fire of 1676. Revere was twice married and raised eleven children. The large family fit into this dwelling, which at the time included a third floor (since removed to restore the building to its original appearance).

ABOVE: The commander at the U.S. Naval Base at the Boston Navy Yard enjoys elegant quarters. OPPOSITE: Actors from the USS Constitution Museum's living-history program "Tales of the USS Constitution"—left to right, Michele Proude as Anne Hull, Brian Turner as George Sirian, and Rose-Ann San Martino as Mrs. Broaders—pose by the ship's bow. The museum is located adjacent to "Old Ironsides" in the Charlestown Navy Yard. The ship, built in 1797 at Boston's Hartt's Shipyard, is the oldest commisioned vessel in the U.S. Navy—and, in fact, the oldest in the world. It was undefeated in battles against pirates off North Africa's Barbary Coast, and again against the British in the War of 1812. On Independence Day each year and on special occasions, it still takes a tour of the harbor, firing its cannons in celebration.

The ornate 1854 Five Cents Savings Bank Building (above) in Charlestown was originally a Masonic hall. Charlestown—now part of Boston—was founded in 1629, a year before Boston. The entire port town was razed by the British in the Revolutionary War. Several fine yachts still berth at the Boston Waterfront Marina (right) at Long Wharf. The New England Aquarium (overleaf) is located at Central Wharf. The aquarium features the world's largest observation tank—a 187,000-gallon, four-story structure in which some of the more than two thousand species swim. Feeding time—five times a day—is not just a surface operation; divers take morsels right to the animals. There's a floating marine mammal pavilion, and the aquarium sponsors whale-watching cruises offshore.

Outside Boston's Computer Museum and Children's Museum, display art turns functional at an ice-cream stand inside a giant Hood's Milk Bottle (above). In the Children's Museum (right), exhibits include a hands-on depiction of aquatic life "Under the Dock." The fifteen-hundred-square-foot exhibit—one of a series with environmental themes—simulates the underwater landscape of Fort Point Channel, complete with a fourteen-foot fiberglass lobster, a dockside puppet theater, barnacle-encrusted dock pilings, and tanks of live lobsters and sea squirts. OVERLEAF: Restaurants and fish markets like the Barking Crab line the Fan Pier across the Northern Bridge. They offer a stellar view of downtown Boston.

A lush, idyllic lagoon (left), lined with weeping willows and other exotic trees, is the centerpiece of the Public Garden, which was created in 1837 as a decorative, flowery, Victorian-style park specifically designed for langorous meandering. The garden was created over what had been Back Bay salt marshes. Swan boats (above), which have glided atop the lagoon since 1877, were created by Robert Paget, an English immigrant and Boston shipbuilder. He was inspired by Richard Wagner's opera Lohengrin, *in which a boat drawn by swans carries the hero across a river. The pedal-powered boats carry tourists past real (and often hungry) ducks, geese, and, occasionally, swans.*

Now the city's most recognizable landmark is the John Hancock Tower (opposite), an I. M. Pei creation that took the name of a 1947 building of the same name. (The latter still stands, its weather beacon steadfastly alerting Bostonians according to an old refrain: "Clear blue, clear view;/ Flashing blue, clouds due;/ Steady red, rain ahead;/ Flashing red, snow ahead.") The newer, sixty-two-story glass rhomboid contains 10,344 "lights" of glass, each weighing five hundred pounds. Every one was replaced after several panes shattered and fell. Hancock security guards used to stand watch on the old building's roof, alert for telltale signs that another pane was in danger of exploding. The rooftops of fashionable Newbury Street row houses (left) form a dramatic contrast to the looming tower.

31

WINCHESTER · 1862 · CEDAR MOUNTAIN ·
ANTIETAM · CHANCELLORSVILLE ·
GETTYSBURG · RESACA · ATLANTA ·
THE MARCH TO THE SEA · SAVANNAH ·
SHERMAN'S CAROLINA CAMPAIGN ·

Phillips Brooks, who composed the Christmas carol "O Little Town of Bethlehem," was rector when the massive new Trinity Church (opposite) was completed. Across Copley Square, stone lions (above) inside the entrance hall of McKim, Mead & White's 1895 Boston Public Library main building salute Massachusetts regiments in the Civil War. Outside, wrought-iron lanterns (overleaf) illuminate the entrance. Sculptor Daniel Chester French designed the building's massive bronze doors. Inside, in the room where books were once delivered to browsers via a tiny train, are murals depicting The Quest of the Holy Grail *and* The Triumph of Time. *Into the building's parapets, the names of 519 important persons in the history of civilization have been carved (the artisans mistakenly repeated four of the names). The library's courtyard contains a fountain, a reflecting pool, and plenty of places to sit and read.*

Commonwealth Avenue, or simply "Comm Av," as Bostonians refer to it, is a wide, restful boulevard of brownstones and other elegant townhouses (right and overleaf). The avenue's mall, extending westward from the Public Garden, continues the "Emerald Necklace," the interconnected Boston park system designed by the "father of landscape architecture," Frederick Law Olmsted. The Comm Av mall makes a picturesque front yard for the avenue's fortunate residents. OPPOSITE: On Newbury Street, "Boston's Madison Avenue" in the Back Bay, creative director James David Bennette, architectural muralist Joshua Winer, and master painter Jack Keledjian created a gigantic, fanciful mural around the corner from the DuBarry French restaurant. It depicts some of history's most famous personages, including, under the left umbrella, Henry Wadsworth Longfellow, and under the right, Babe Ruth.

On streets like
Warren Street
(right), the eclectic
South End is full
of what Bostonians
call "bowfronts"—
buildings whose bay
windows reach all the
way from ground to
roof level. Most were
constructed in the
1850s, when the Back
Bay to the north was
still mainly a bog,
separated from the
South End by a series
of railroad tracks.
Originally a pleasant
Victorian neighbor-
hood built on landfill
around The Neck—
a narrow strip of
land that, amazingly,
was once the only
land approach to
Boston—the South
End deteriorated
badly before enjoy-
ing a revitalization
in the 1990s. Even
today it is a neighbor-
hood for the upwardly
mobile, where
students and young
couples get a start.
Though Tremont
Street is a major
traffic and business
artery, it has blocks of
handsome residences
(opposite) as well.

Boston's old trolleys still run along Huntington Avenue in the South End (above). South Boston—not to be confused with the South End—is full of warehouses (right), produce and fish companies, restaurants, and museums. Fenway Park (overleaf) is one of baseball's most historic ballparks. It seats only 34,000 fans, most of whom get a close-up view of the action. The park's "Green Monster," just 315 feet from home plate, tempts right-handed batters and bedevils left-handed pitchers. Yet two of the hometown Red Sox's greatest batters— Ted Williams and Carl Yazstremski— hit left-handed. So did one of baseball's greatest sluggers, Babe Ruth, but he was a pitcher in Boston, and the Sox traded him to the Yankees before his career blossomed.

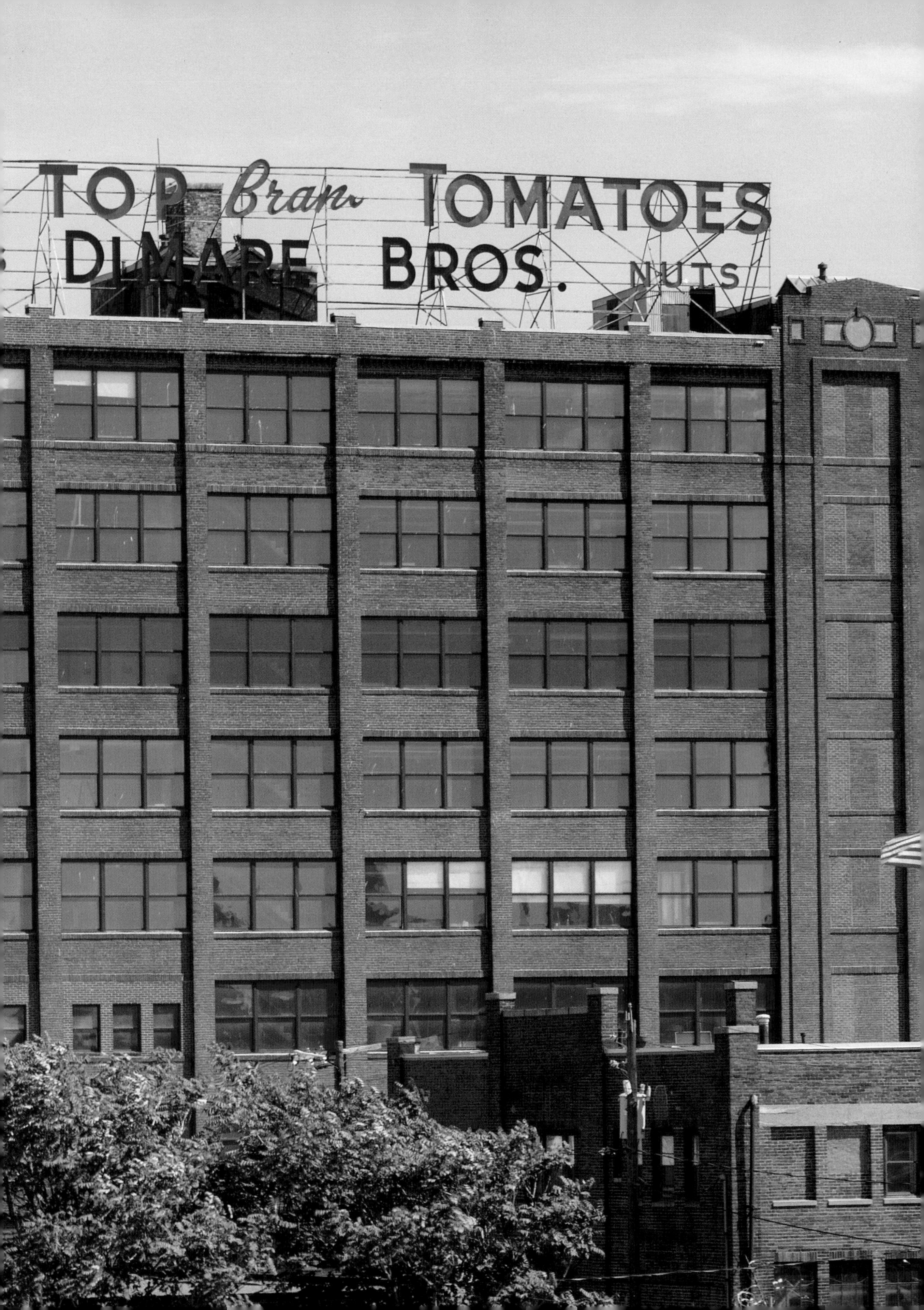
TOP Bran TOMATOES
DIMARE BROS.
NUTS

Flamboyant Boston hostess Isabella Stewart Gardner unveiled her private art collection at the Fenway Court (left) in her new Venetian-style villa in 1903. When she died in 1924, her will stipulated that all of the artwork remain displayed exactly as it was at that time, or else it would all be sold and the proceeds turned over to Harvard University. To date, the Isabella Stewart Gardner Museum remains open in Boston's Fenway section. Nearly two thousand objects are on display in Veronese, Dutch, Titian, and other rooms. OPPOSITE: Boston's Museum of Fine Arts, one of the nation's finest art repositories, moved to the Fenway in 1909. Hometown artist John Singleton Copley is one of several American masters whose work is featured here. Its collection of Asian art is the largest under one roof in the world.

RIGHT: A sculpture in front of Boston University's Ralph Adams Cram Chapel honors Martin Luther King Jr., who earned his doctorate degree at the nation's fifth-largest private university. OPPOSITE: Tall reeds, two attractive bridges, community "victory garden" plots, three war memorials, and several sports fields can be found in the marshy Back Bay Fens. This area was a stinking repository of sewage runoff until landscape architect Frederick Law Olmstead was brought in to transform it into "public pleasure gardens." Sculling is a passion all along the Charles River (overleaf). Not far from this John W. Weeks footbridge are several boathouses where Harvard and other university students practice almost year-round for spirited competitions.

The striking tower of Dunster House dormitory (right) is one of many landmarks on the Harvard University campus. None is more symbolic of scholarship than Widener Library on Harvard Yard (opposite and overleaf), completed by African-American architect Julian Francis Abele, who had also designed the Widener family mansion in Newport, R.I. The library honors family patriarch Harry Elkins Widener, who died aboard the Titanic. *The library houses the second-largest collection of books in America (behind only the Library of Congress), including a Gutenberg Bible and a Shakespeare folio. Harvard boasts two art museums and a huge museum of cultural and natural history.*

Boston's Museum of Science, which straddles the Charles River dam in the city's old West End, features more than four hundred exhibits but is perhaps best known for its twenty-foot-high model of Tyrannosaurus Rex *(above)*. Massachusetts Institute of Technology was relocated from a downtown campus (where it was known as Boston Tech) to landfill atop a marsh across the Charles River at the start of the twentieth century. MIT graduate William Welles Bosworth designed the university's signature Maclaurin Building *(right)*. MIT's campus is just as bustling as Harvard's upriver, though more prosaic, practical, and less picturesque, architecturally. Its profusion of laboratories earned it the nickname "The Factory."

Sedate Brookline offers a surprising attraction in the carriage house of the old Larz and Isabel Anderson estate. It's a compact museum of transportation, featuring many of Larz Anderson's collection of thirty-three automobiles. Thanks to additional donations such as a 1909 Locomobile (above), known as "the best-built car in America," the collection now tops two hundred vintage cars. Larz Anderson was a U.S. ambassador to Japan; Isabel wrote wildly popular children's stories. RIGHT: On Beals Street in Brookline stands the home where John F. Kennedy was born on May 29, 1917. Four of Joseph and Rose Kennedy's nine children were born in the modest house in the years when the elder Kennedy began to amass a fortune as a financier.

A Boston visit often includes a journey to Revolutionary War sites in nearby Lexington and Concord. The "Line of the Minute Men, April 19, 1775" is remembered in an 1892 statue on the Lexington Common (right), where a Captain Parker is supposed to have said, "Stand your guard. Don't fire until fired upon. But if they mean to have a war, let it begin here." At the Old North Bridge in Concord (opposite), Minute Men fired the shot heard 'round the world that inflicted the Revolution's first British casualties. Tranquillity is the mood at Walden Pond (overleaf) near Concord, where swimming and fishing have replaced transcendentalist Henry David Thoreau's contemplation in a one-room cabin on the shoreline, and conservationists have successfully kept commercial development at bay.

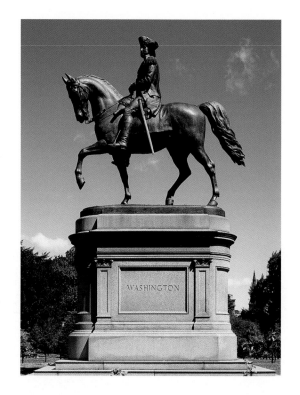

Titles available in the Pictorial Souvenir series